Build Your
Human
Equity
Line
Of
Credit™

*The Secrets to Creating a Lifetime of
Assets in ANY Economy*

Steven E. LaBroi

Published by LaBroi Insurance Group, LLC
www.labroiinsurancegroup.com

Scripture quotation is taken from THE NEW KING JAMES VERSION of the Bible. Copyright © 1979, 1980, 1982 Thomas Nelson, Inc., Publishers.

Human Equity Line of Credit is a registered trademark of Steven E. LaBroi.

ISBN: 978-0-9834354-4-0 (paperback)
Book Cover & Interior Design by TWA Solutions.com
Library of Congress Control Number: 2018912195

LIMITS OF LIABILITY/DISCLAIMER OF WARRANTY

*I dedicate this book to
my mother, Mary LaBroi, and my grandmother, Ethel Coffey.
They raised me to think openly and honestly about life,
allowing me to grow as a man and professional, while
being supportive with no judgment.*

Acknowledgments

I want to acknowledge my friend and book mentor, Jessica Tilles, for encouraging me to write a book and to get my thoughts on paper.

To my grandmother, Rosella LaBroi, for being a super advocate for education.

To my grandfathers, Duel Coffey, Sr. and Lester LaBroi, Sr., for being examples of strength and discipline

To my dad, Lester LaBroi, Jr., for instilling in me the persistence and the drive to go after what I want.

To my uncles, Michael LaBroi, Jerome LaBroi, Leonard Coffey, James Gaston, Duel Coffey Jr., and my aunt, Karen LaBroi, who have always cheered for me in anything I have done.

To my sister, Corey LaBroi, and nephews, Jaden and Justen, along with brothers Les, Blake, and Kyle, and all my cousins and family who watched me grow from afar.

To my friends from near and far, who have heard my cry for entrepreneurship and dreams of being in business for myself from my days at Nursery Land Foundation (Eloise Gentry) to now.

To Dr. Edwin Chapman, Royce Peters, Damon Wilson, Charles Murray, Ulysses Glee and the Fenton Family, C.F. Jackson, Stephen Russell, Ross Haith Jr., Steve McKenzie, Tess and Timothy George, Tyra Wright, Blane Smith, Angela Borden, Kristie Walton, Troy and Shannon Datcher, Jeffrey Pugh, Stacy Harrison, Emanuel and Pamela Payton, Twanda Black, Tyrone and Toni Banks, Denecia Abear, Kelly S. Adams, Charles Cox, Charlotte Comer, Shirley Grant, Karen D. Smith, Adrienne Turner, Kimberly O'Shields, and Cornelius "Petey" Crockett. You all have been an integral part of my entrepreneurial journey.

To my classmates and teachers at Theodore Roosevelt High School, Gary, Indiana for every class "Dearly Loved." Also, to my entire GI (Gary, Indiana) village, which I often called my cocoon teaching me the values, morals, leadership, and discipline to survive in the world loving everyone from the "crib".

Finally, thanks to J.D. Shields for opening my eyes to this strategy and the idea of changing lives.

To my Morehouse College classmates and professors, who still drive me to reach for the "Crown," I watch you all in awe and in brotherhood as we all strive to serve mankind set forth by our motto "et facta est lux."

This book is my truth and my light found by years of searching for a way to help mankind and, most of all my culture, to see a way clear for current and future generations. This is a way of bringing the past, present, and future together to methodically move into ourselves. I called it being POSITIVELY SELFISH. By merging the words "positive" and "selfish," you begin to see a way of focusing on you and your family while not being pulled into the world at-large. We have gone from an intimate familial world to what is preached and drilled into us as a GLOBAL society. How can one ever make a mark and build a legacy through your family by always satisfying the global world first? We must get back to creating traditions and educating our generations in a way that they will take the story forward. Tell the "Roots" story of your family so the future has a chance at building on the foundation your parents and grandparents set. In personal finance, I believe we can set new traditions without excuses. I challenge us today to begin to unlearn, learn, and teach different ways of building wealth to our children and ourselves. This is done simply by using the global messaging tool—the Internet. There are no more excuses of information not being available. We have the information in the palm of our hands. The Bible says to seek the knowledge. Now we can teach locally to prepare ourselves and our future generations to be able to manage globally off a foundation set by us. WE ARE THE LEGACY CHANGE GENERATION, no matter what age you are now. You are a part of the legacy change generation because there is nothing that will hold you back from learning except your own personal restriction of allowing your mind to open. Information is everywhere.

It is my hope that for those that read this book that it begins to open a dialogue of conscientious thought on another way of managing money. Peace be with you and your family while you build your financial foundation!

Table of Contents

INTRODUCTION

"You are your greatest asset. Put your time, effort and money into training, grooming, and encouraging your greatest asset."

–Tom Hopkins

When most people think of assets, they think of money, cars, houses, land, jewelry and other material possessions. I love the above quote by Tom Hopkins, an international sales and management trainer, because it helps me to paint the picture I hope you will visualize after reading this book. YOU are your greatest ASSET! I encounter people who don't know their value. It is my passion to help you build YOU first. You will become positively selfish. The word selfish is usually related to being negative, but we want everyone to build their wealth, net worth, and assets, at which time you will be in a much better place to help all those you want.

There is an epidemic convincing people they have to work themselves to death to obtain the American dream; working endless hours to rob Peter to pay Paul at the end of each week and often Paul does not get paid.

There are people who cannot afford an emergency in the form of illness or even a car breaking down because they may or may not have the funds for deductibles or repairs.

Having little or no money will never stop life from happening. Life will happen whether you have one dollar or one million dollars. So, how do you move from struggling financially toward financial independence? Some may say, "Win the lottery" or "Rob a bank." The chances at winning the lottery are slim and robbing a bank will land you in prison. Build a business or work a career to bring in income. Well, I have an idea that will take a little sacrifice, dedication, commitment, habit changes, and the willingness to be better. If you know better, you do better, not only for today, but also for generations to come.

Let me introduce you to the HUMAN Equity Line of Credit™ (HuE-LOC). Not to confuse with a Home Equity Line of Credit (HELOC), which you secure through a bank. A HUMAN Equity Line of Credit™ (HuE-LOC) is a means of providing wealth for your current and future spending by using YOU as the collateral. Tom Hopkins said it best when he said, *"This is the opportunity to put your time, money, and effort toward something that will build a huge asset over time."* I want to partner with you to provide the steps and training on how this over 100 year old strategy can work for you...if you work it.

Now, I get it. We live in a microwave mentality society. We want everything quick, fast, and easy. I have learned that anything worth having is worth working for and building upon. It does not mean you wait forever. If you are ready to build wealth and create a legacy for generations to come, continue reading as I break down the 13 valuable steps that paint a more vivid picture of building a HUMAN Equity Line of Credit.

You are the Collateral

You are the Collateral

alued as an asset, collateral is something you pledge as security for repayment of a loan that you forfeit if you default. For example, an asset could be any property you own, cash in a savings account, or a 401(k) retirement plan. With a Human Equity Line of Credit™ (HuE-LOC), you are the collateral, which allows you to be in complete control of your funds. Your age, health, income, and stage of life is the basis for building your HuE-LOC strategy.

You serve as the nucleus of the strategy and no financing institution will tell you how, when, or what to do concerning the goals of your HuE-LOC.

Let's take a closer look at this!

If you have a HELOC, the economy and financial industry can determine your outcomes. A financial institution's evaluation determines the value of your home. For example, if your home has a mortgage loan, which is usually the first loan debt on your home, a lender or financial institution has to review it. Your home has to meet a mortgage company/lender's underwriting criteria to be eligible for a second loan/equity line of credit for you to leverage.

In addition, there are several other factors to consider:

- The economy has to be right for lending.
- The home value has to be right.
- The neighborhood has to be right.
- The interest rates have to be right.
- Your credit score has to be right.
- Your bills have to be right.
- Your smile has to be right with the lender (just kidding).

However, with a HuE-LOC, you can strategize your goals based on a set of factors you determine. You build *your* bank of funds *you* can use for *anything with no restrictions*. A HuE-LOC provides tax-free benefits and very flexible terms of use. There is also protection for your family wealth/income, and protection from creditors trying to get to your funds through collections, judgments, or lawsuits.

Build Guaranteed Savings Toward *Current* and *Future* Spending

Build Guaranteed Savings Toward *Current* and *Future* Spending

2

This is an age-old, effective concept our family elders used. Unlike today, they used this concept because they didn't have access to instant money. They were not fortunate to have credit cards, debit cards, ATMs, check-cashing stores, cash for cars, PayPal, Venmo Apps, Cash Apps, and the list goes on. Their only option was to save, save, save! Since life is full of surprises, this concept has never failed. On average, Americans only save three percent or less of their income for a rainy day (emergency, lifestyle, retirement). If you are a saver, you know what it is like to be prepared for that rainy day. If it has not rained in your life yet, just keep living.

One major goal should be to strive to have a guaranteed cushion in place to prepare for life's unexpected events, expected circumstances, and inevitable wants and/or needs. Money makes the world go around and cashflow is always needed. Overall, the government prints and spends money; consumers make and spend money, and companies profit off what consumers spend while providing jobs so this cycle can continue. This should balance out the economy, or so we expect it to. We know the economy will fall short and we may not be ready.

Every day there is the temptation to spend money through television ads, Internet, cellphones, newspaper advertisements, and billboards, which I call white noise that drowns out strategies and thoughts. The push for new ways to advertise to Americans continues to grow. In addition, there is the must-spend for food, clothing, and shelter. Please understand that spending is an emotional exercise. It occurs through conscientious and unconscientious ways which triggers our consumer gene. We cannot live without spending. The cost of living increases every year, so it can get very expensive to live in today's world. Look at the cost of any item and see how it continues to rise. Spending becomes an issue when there are wants or needs and the resources are not available. This attributes to our habits and discipline. People who have access to a constant flow of funds tend not to worry unless they cannot control their habits, emotions, and discipline. The amount of money you make does not change your habits you can be broke at any income. Making more money may not be the answer. However, what about those who don't have a way of creating regular funds or the white noise does distracts them? What about the person who has bad credit and cannot get funds in case of an emergency? We tend not to consider these things until situations or circumstances arise. This is the time to consider having access to funds from one day to the next; we have no idea of what could take place.

Preparation, strategy, and goal setting are a few keys toward financial security and success! You can gain this security by building a HuE-LOC. It is a guarantee that you will build a nice little nest egg of funds for current and future spending through this method a HuE-LOC.

Savings is nothing more than delayed spending, whether it's impulsive, emotional, peer pressure-driven, a habit, lifestyle—real or perceived—and anything else you do. Spending is an activity driven by emotions to provide personal satisfaction.

The big question is, "Does your savings guarantee spending for current and future expenditures for the rest of your life?" Maybe you are like many who ride the roller coaster of spending that pushes and pulls them through the tracks of life. Maybe you are neither and you are financially literate with a game plan, both now and for the future. Maybe you are a network marketer and expect residual income forever. However, even then, a HuE-LOC can create more efficiency with funds, even securing the use for generations to come.

Do you want to create a better, more efficient way in any economy? A HuE-LOC is a guaranteed strategy that will assist individuals or business owners to build a lifetime of wealth that, if set up correctly through available agreements and strategies, could benefit you through retirement, your children, and even your grandchildren. Now, who would not want to learn to do that? If you don't have children, then you should create wealth that will help you throughout your life, ultimately passing it down to your alma mater, organization, church, community, etc. We should build wealth within our families and communities. We can do this by creating HuE-LOCs.

My client, Betty, believes in saving, living below her means, and paying off her bills. After paying off debt, she does not squander the extra money she now has. Instead, she is building her wealth by saving it every month. Since she has at least twelve years until retirement, building her wealth now will allow her to have funds available when she needs it. She is creating her own bank of funds.

Instead of stashing her extra money between the mattress or in a cookie jar, she deposits it every month into her credit union savings account. Since the 2008 banking/mortgage crisis, we are living in low-interest times, which means most banks are paying very little (one percent, if we're lucky) on deposits. Therefore, most savers are seeing little to nothing on their deposits, in the name of interest. By law, all interest earned on savings accounts is taxable, even if only a few dollars or cents. Meanwhile, the banks make its money on higher interest loans.

Although Betty is consistent with depositing money into her savings account, she isn't earning enough interest to make it worth her while. Therefore, I suggested she move her money out of a system that pays little to no interest and exposes her to taxes (and even creditors). I showed Betty how to become her own HuE-LOC by placing her dollars into a system that not only gets her more in interest but the additional protection and potential dividends will allow her to see a significant growth through her retirement timeframe. In addition, she will have access to her money as it grows—TAX-FREE.

Remember, money has to reside somewhere. Find the optimal place to put it so it will benefit you in *any* economy.

Build Assets to Supply Your Income Needs for Your Future

Build Assets to Supply Your Income Needs for Your Future

3

A n "asset" is *a useful or valuable object, person, or quality with value; it is also real property owned by a person or entity, having value, which you can also use to leverage debts, commitments, and build legacies.* Many people believe their home is an asset. Property is a valuable asset, which you can use as such when the value is positive, however, it is not a liquid asset. A liquid asset is cash-on-hand or an asset you can readily convert to cash. You can only get funds from your property upon approval from the lender as a second mortgage or the complete sale of the property. With a second mortgage, stipulations such as appraisals, income, credit, debt, economy, and values will apply. The lender maintains the property as collateral. An asset can be a rental or vacation property, which is an investment property when someone else pays for the mortgage, maintenance, and liability through the payment of rent. However, even if you paid the mortgage in full and own the property out right showing the asset on your balance sheet as part of your net worth the property can only be a liquid asset if it is sold or a loan is requested from the bank using it as collateral. But, don't forget that you must pay taxes, insurance, and possibly home owners association fees, if required.

There is so much to consider, but I will teach you how to build a different asset that is liquid from *Day 1*. It does not require a million steps and you do not have to be a certain age to leverage this tool as a wealth-building asset. You can leverage it personally or through your business by borrowing while it still compounds interest. This is an opportunity to build an asset you control and not the *banks*. With a HuE-LOC, *you* become the *bank*!

My friend, Richard, is always looking to build assets. He definitely believes in Robert Kiyosaki, the author of *Rich Dad, Poor Dad*, and his theory of amassing assets and allowing them to pay you passively throughout your life. However, when I spoke with Richard recently, we discussed his large real estate holdings and that although he was happy with the passive income from his rental properties, he realized he did not have control over the assets.

During our conversation, Richard expressed his concerns. "Brother, I don't own these assets since I have mortgages with several banks and, even if I pay them off, I still have to pay insurance and taxes. In addition, if I sell them, I lose the income and possibly have a tax bill in front of me, depending on the economy and tax laws we are living under at that time. Congress can change anything when it feels like it and I can't do anything about it. Is there an asset that is liquid, and grows, throws off money, is protected from creditors and taxes, I can leverage as collateral and build my net worth?"

Now, I love real estate. It has proven to be an avenue toward building wealth. In fact, people have become millionaires from real estate. Even I dabble in it, but how do they control it overall without everybody's hands involved.

As I explained to Richard, it is hard to keep everybody's hands out of your pockets. However, he could consider other assets that work alongside real estate holdings that would give him contractual control. Assets that he could customize its size and have access to the money while controlling the taxes staying in line with the IRS. Also, he could even create a stronghold to keep the dollars out of the hands of creditors, in case of any business downturns.

With a HuE-LOC, you can balance out your needs of having to go to a financial institution for everything you do and having to prove you are creditworthy. Banks want to deal with people with money and usually, the people that need banks are people who *need* money. Banks are very particular to people who need money, thus creating restrictive guidelines. However, financial institutions want to give their money to people with money so they can be more assured to get that money back with interest. Their job is to *sell money* to someone they think will pay it back with interest and without issues.

While Richard has a good business model, he needs to count how much money he is BUYING from the bank and how much they have PROFITED from those loans.

Let's put you in Richard's shoes. What if you could be the bank? What if you could buy and renovate your properties, using your own money? What if you didn't have to pay a bank during the construction phase? What if you could pay yourself back with interest with some of the same tax deductions and write-offs coming to you as if you were the bank? This is what having a HuE-LOC is all about, being your own financial institution in control of your life in any economy. Even during retirement, you control your finances in your senior years based on taxes and healthcare cost because you would have the dollars to use and assets not viewed as income by the IRS.

If the 2008 financial crisis told us anything, it told us that even the US economy is not dependable. However, being your own bank is reliable. You have to look into other options and be open to other possibilities right alongside standard financial risk practices.

Never Worry About *Finding Finances* for Your Business Again

Never Worry About *Finding Finances* For Your Business Again

4

ntrepreneurship is on a steady rise. Starting a new business and becoming your own boss is an exciting, exhilarating idea, but it can also be scary. Regardless of the type of business, it takes capital to get it started. Even a home-based business requires some amount of capital. You would have to get the word out about your business, which requires marketing and promotions, and that takes money. You have to pay for the operations of your business, which also takes money. Even if you market through social media buying ads becomes an option.

Having a vision for a business is one thing, but finding the capital for the business is another. Most of us, if we don't have our own savings or credit cards we are willing to burn through, have to look to outside sources for capital. In the nineties, it was called OPM (other people's money), which was a move to either find investors or borrow money as a loan from an institution, or maybe even friends and family to use as seed funds for a business. Through these methods, you are beholding to the lender or funding source by a contract or equity ownership in your company. You can lose your business if you don't pay the money back. Unless we have a rich uncle who willingly gives up money to spend without paying it back, an angel investor. we all must consider the risk. Money is the number one issue to manage business operations, forecasting longevity, keeping employees employed, buying and managing inventory, and finally producing profit. Many people shy away from the idea of entrepreneurship because they are already robbing Peter to pay Paul to maintain their basic everyday needs. Borrowing a large sum of money to try out an idea only to have someone else in control is a fearful thought. However, if entrepreneurship is bubbling in your veins, we have an answer to those issues. You need a strategy. Yes, there is an alternate way to accumulate and maintain funding for your company and it begins with building a HuE-LOC right along with building the business.

It is typical for a business to reinvest revenues/profits to prevent having a deficit of capital and to run operations for the upcoming months. Some companies even have an investment arm that make money with the profits of the company. They build the safety net for the company in case of a business decision gone awry or a new product introduction. Always needing more money. The goal is to eventually run the business operations without relying on bank loans or investors. A business needs capital to grow to sustain rough times, changes in the economy, competition in business, seasonality of the business, and new marketing ideas. Businesses need a HuE-LOC strategy also.

Once you accumulate capital using the HuE-LOC strategy, you will have the option of lending money to your business, repaying you the bank, and even enjoying some of the tax benefits afforded by a lending institution when lending to you in a normal borrowing environment. With a HuE-LOC, you can eliminate the bank and even Peter and Paul. In the same manner, as banks and financial institutions, you have the freedom to create your own terms for your business regarding funding. You can proactively manage finances to your benefit operating your business to win. Your business pays you back the loan with interests, per your agreement. This will allow you to grow your bank of funds to be able to loan again and again protecting your businesses future need for capital. This is true capitalization of your own business. You can use this strategy as many times as needed and it keeps you in control of not having to borrow from financial institutions.

I know this may sound too good to be true. However, it is true. A proven strategy spanning many years, it is an age-old idea of planning and saving, anticipating that the future is a part of our lives. A HuE-LOC has the tools to use to get it done. What are you waiting for? Let's get started building your Human Equity Line of Credit, (HuE-LOC). The time is *now!*

As an entrepreneur, John has owned a brick and mortar retail business for ten years. He has had his ups and downs with the market and the economy. Internet retailing has been tough on brick and mortar businesses, causing many to go out of business. John knows he has to make some decisions to find an exit strategy, take his business online, where he has in-store sales through online advertising, or sell products directly online with fulfillment and shipping directly to a larger customer base. Although the U.S. Supreme Court is beginning an assault on taxes for online sales via state rules, retailers who want to survive still must figure out the Internet game and, at best, the social media marketing game to keep eyeballs on their products and services.

So, my client, John, who has purchased disability insurance from me, is searching for a way to finance these new ways of staying in business. He knows it is tough to go to the bank with no real collateral unless he puts up his home as collateral or if his business has a great Dunn and Bradstreet credit score. He may be able to get signature loans or merchant sales loans based on cash register receipts, both of which carry heavy interest and penalties if you cannot pay. He has some cash flow and manages his business with his bookkeeper, but he needs to make sure he has accessible money in case of emergencies and ultimately retirement.

We discussed building a High Cash Value Whole Life insurance policy, where it works several ways. John can earn interest on his money above commercial bank rates, he has access to the money when needed for emergencies, business or anything, and he will receive non-guaranteed dividends in his account if the company does well. I was able to customize his contract so he gets the most out of his policy, including tax write-offs for borrowing the money and paying it back.

John can borrow against his policy from the insurance companies' general fund and not have to repay the loan until he is ready and at the amount he chooses, giving him time to test a couple strategies with online marketing. Now, if he uses other financing, they will dictate the terms and the pressure is much greater to succeed or face the consequence of collections, bad credit, judgments, and even going out of business if he doesn't do well.

Some people still believe in OPM (other people's money). To those people, I offer this: Imagine how better you will feel to have complete control over the money *you* work hard to earn. You have all the leverage when you put up all the money and win. Leverage is also when you control all decisions in the business.

Keep *Compound Interest* Growing Even While Using Your *Funds*

Keep *Compound Interest* Growing Even While Using Your *Funds*

5

"Compound interest is the eighth wonder of the world. He who understands it earns it... he who doesn't... pays it."
– Albert Einstein

nterest is money earned each day, each month, and each year and is added to your principal dollars when invested or promised by a financial product you find to invest your money. Banks pay interest on deposits of funds in particular products based on you leaving your money in those accounts over time.

Webster defines *interest* as *a charge for borrowed money generally a percentage of the amount borrowed or the profit made on invested money.* Remember what we just said about banks are they really paying us interest to borrow our money? Think about it. Banks then lend our money to others and us for a higher interest. Things that make you go *hmmm*. We will keep exploring this subject.

Compound interest, when added to the principal, doesn't merely grow, it grows at an ever-increasing rate, which is one of the most powerful concepts in finance. However, do you use it to its fullest potential, or when you borrow money, are you paying a lot of it to someone else? When it comes to your money, on which side do you focus on? The HuE-LOC strategy focuses on the growth and use of your money while your interest compounds continuously, which financial institutions do not do. A great goal can be to control the use of your funds, never lose those funds, protect those funds, earn potential dividends on those funds, and pass along those funds, tax-free, to your family and next generation, all while the interest is still compounding.

The IRS has sanctioned the use of such a tool and it has been in use for over one hundred years. Commercial banks, major corporations and many families use this tool to create generational wealth. In fact, a few founders of major corporations like Walmart, Disney, and J.C. Penney used this tool to keep their businesses afloat or to test market strategies when no banks would lend them money. What if no one will lend you money, but then you can lend money to yourself and have all those other benefits described above?

Banks, financing companies, and even insurance companies do not want you to know about this strategy. They are all in the business of selling you money to make interest for their pockets. They are major institutions trying to make a profit. However, if you learn this strategy you can rest your money in this account and use it for anything you want while it still compounds and you can put the money back and do it repeatedly. Fact is the benefits are intrinsic in the contracts/policies you just have to be taught the secrets on setting them up. You have to ask yourself why you do not see this promoted on television. A little over 100,000 clients and 1% of agents are aware of this strategy. Agents who practice this type of program take a cut in commission to help these clients benefit. It takes a special agent to teach this strategy. It is time to put your hand in the cookie jar to pull out a cookie and not the leftover crumbs! It's all in the strategy.

Mark always wondered why the system never seemed to be in his favor. As a finance major, he always wondered why financial institutions that held his money in their accounts made more money than he did in interests for using his money. Additionally, when he invested in other vehicles that were supposed to pay him more, there were more risks involved. Not only the risk but the potential taxes as well. He soon realized he could lose it all or win it all. Then there was the economy that he could not affect at all, he had to react to circumstances as they occur.

Mark did not work in investments and banking every day to keep an eye on his money, so he had to trust someone else to make money for him. He realized that when he put money in an institution or with a broker he had no control over its wins or losses and even the ability to use the money when necessary. Also, no one would help him with an exit strategy as to when to pull his money out. It just stayed in to go up and down based on the brokers work or non-work. This just makes Mark feel helpless.

Mark had to find a system that benefited him more. He searched Google for a solution and found a little-known strategy, but an old strategy from an old industry. Surprised, he learned life insurance was the vehicle that would solve his problem. A tool to use that allows you to have a place to put money and it works in more than one way.

Tax-free *Use* and Tax-free *Growth* of Your Funds. Who would have known?

Tax-free *Use* and Tax-free *Growth* of Your Funds. Who would have known?

6

Are you a part of the crowd who hates paying taxes or even hearing the word tax? Are you a part of the crowd that looks at taxes as a foregone conclusion like paying tax on cable bills, cell phones, rental cars or any other sales tax? Most people fall in one of these categories while others focus on tax deductions as it relates to business expenses or homeownership. People talk about interest deductions in their home mortgages as a tax write-off or writing off their children as a deduction as a coveted benefit. What if you could manage taxes by simply placing money in an account that has tax-free to use and provides tax-free growth while you are earning interest? To plan and build a part of your portfolio to have tax-free use and tax-free growth means you are able to decide, in some situations, if you want to pay taxes. Now, you will still have to pay sales tax, income tax, or tax to your cable bill monthly and your cell phone company, but to be able to grow and use your personal money tax-free is way cool, and it is all in the Internal Revenue Service's Tax Code as of the writing of this book. If you did not know? Keep reading.

The government sanctioned these variables and the IRS approved rules around it, along with a Government Accountancy Office whitepaper presented January 1990 called "Tax Policy Tax treatment of Life Insurance and Annuity Accrued Interest." The document studied the benefits and effects on the interest build up and use of those funds in cash value life insurance and annuities. Before the IRS ruling, life insurance and annuities were used not only for benefits to your families in case of loss of income but also used to grow money through insurance companies in many customized ways. The current rules establish a line between life insurance and investing. Modified Endowment Contract a MEC line is the line or amount of cash that can be put in a policy before it will be considered an investment. In the GAO Whitepaper, it states, "The interest you earn on life insurance policies and deferred annuity contracts are commonly referred to as "inside buildup," and are not taxed as long as it accumulates within the contract. By choosing not to tax the interest as you earn it, the federal government forgoes an estimated five *billion* dollars in tax revenue each year."[1]

The secret is how to get the inside buildup out as it accumulates and be able to use it for you and your family.

If a policyholder borrows the inside buildup from a life insurance policy, the amount borrowed is considered a transfer

---

[1]United States Government Accounting Office (GAO), January 1990 Tax Policy, Tax Treatment of Life Insurance and Annuity Accrued Interest.

of capital, not a realization of income, and, therefore is not subject to taxation. This reasoning is in accord with tax policy on other types of loans, such as consumer loans or home mortgages. These loans are merely transfers of capital or savings from one person to another through a financial intermediary. The ability to borrow against a life insurance policy means the interest income that is supposed to be building up to fund the death benefits can instead be a source of untaxed current income. If the loans are not repaid, the inside buildup will never be taxed; death benefits will simply be reduced by the amount of the loan. Thus, policyholders have the use of tax-free income for the purposes other than insurance at the expense of reduced death benefits for their beneficiaries.[2]

There is a difference between each product, life insurance, and annuities in this regard. With a life insurance policy, as long as you don't turn the policy back (surrender it) to the company and you have made a profit on the cash value or owe any money to the life insurance company then you will not be charged a tax. A policyholder can also borrow against their policy from the life insurance company and use the money tax-free. Most people are familiar with borrowing from their life insurance policy. You actually borrow from the life insurance companies general fund. This is one way you can begin to build your HuE-LOC. Yes, I am talking about a whole life insurance product designed

---

[2]United State Government Accounting Office (GAO), January 1990 Tax Policy, Tax Treatment of Life Insurance and Annuity Accrued Interest.

to earn high cash value and potential dividends. These policies are specifically designed to do the things necessary to reach our goals of having lifetime efficient funds we can use for our entire life and pass along to our children and grandchildren. There are many different life insurance policies, so you must check the specific terms of your policies. You may be able to accomplish this with the current policy you have or you may need to discuss this with your agent or an agent who is familiar with the right design. It is all about design and coaching; design the policy for you to fuel your cash value, which will actually decrease the agent's commission. This is why it is so special, and it takes an agent who uses this strategy regularly to help clients.

Annuities are life insurance products and do have an inside buildup of earnings. However, they are taxed when you pull the funds out as profit is earned and can have penalties attached if you pull money before 59½ years of age or before the annuitization period in the contract. Annuities also depend if the funds used to set it up are from qualified funds (401(k), 403(b), 457, etc.) or non-qualified (cash). Remember I said both are contracts, so we must understand each. Both, I will say, play an important role in the HuE-LOC strategy because, during retirement, the need for income is much greater to deal with lifestyle, emergencies, and healthcare. An annuity can be set up to provide income for your *entire* life in a contract with the insurance company with guarantees. We do not want to run out of money while we are living. It's another important role in our strategy to ensure your money outlives you.

Create a HuE-LOC using your 401(k), 457, 403(b), IRA, cash savings or other retirement plans you receive from your employer or financial institutions, as long as you have no major economic changes or no catastrophic health issues. We want you to think strategically instead of just about products by using these private institutions you can accomplish your short-term and long-term goals safely. The government-based programs allow us to postpone taxes, which seems great regarding taxes coming off our monthly paychecks. However, they are only postponing taxes to be paid later, in which it is not determined the amount of taxes you will have to pay. Most people think all the money saved in these programs belong to them until it's time to withdraw it potentially at age 59 ½ or even at 70 ½ and when it's time for a Mandatory withdrawal called the RMD— Required Minimum Distribution. If you don't pay at this time, the government can take up to 50% of that distribution amount in taxes. Therefore, these programs are designed for you to save on taxes early and pay the taxes on it later. You actually need to be aware and plan for that reality, so you are still able to accomplish the same goals for retirement. If the tax rates are high when you defer your money, it is good not to have to pay taxes on income. However, if tax rates are low during this time, such as new marginal tax rates on the tax reform of 2018, and you are deferring money from your paycheck until a later time after these tax rates are over the taxes could be higher. Will taxes be lower or will taxes be higher when you retire?

Most, if not all of these programs, have limits to the amount of money you can defer annually. Business owner programs have larger annual amounts and even they have limits. Once you have reached those limits, you have to take all the money anyway and pay the tax on it today. Even the ROTH IRA and ROTH 401(k), where you pay taxes up-front, have limits. Although they are great, because you don't have to worry about guessing what the taxes will be in the future, if you don't plan to maximize the accounts, you are still shorting yourself with this strategy. Government-based employer and business owner programs will let you delay paying income tax but limit the amount of money you can put in them. This is why you should look to add private institution programs to your HuE-LOC to give you more flexibility, freedom, and control.

Let's create and control the use of your money and grow it safely. Customize your program, consequently managing to your benefit an amount you can use throughout your life and not just for when you retire, but for generations to come.

We hope to live a long time, God willing, and we will need to have and spend money to enjoy it so let's create a HuE-LOC to manage it.

I always ask my clients, "What if you could have money you could use during your lifetime and throughout retirement, while it grows tax-free and still able to leave your children a strong financial foundation when you are gone? Their reply is always, "Sign me up!"

You Don't Always
Have to Pay Interest

You Don't Always
Have to Pay Interest

7

Paying interest is not my favorite thing to do. I don't know about you, but having to pay interest gets under my skin. I call it "buying other people's money." When you get a loan, secure a mortgage, use a credit card, or even utilize a payday cash loan, you are *paying* to use other people's money. Most of us take this for granted. With other people's money comes a payment schedule that includes interest, and based on the type of loan, you might even be paying the interest *before* you start paying on the principle, which means your balances on the actual amount you borrowed may not seem to decrease for a while.

We double and triple pay, or even make more payments during the same month, all to pay off the debt as fast as we can, at times forsaking our own cash flow needs. We can end up in a life where we are just creating a vicious cycle of paying someone else first and buying their money or receiving credit, not paying attention to how much we pay into their profit (interest). They maintain pressure on us based on reporting our payment history to the credit bureaus, forcing us to have to operate under a system where we have little control. Maintaining our credit score will end up being our life's preoccupation to pay someone else for the use of their money. This would be great, if we can manage our income properly and decide we want to use this system to help us in strategic investments to make money. By using other people's money, you are relinquishing control over your own income since you spend most of your time paying interest and principle to another company and not growing it for youself.

Remember, interest is the cost to you for borrowing/*buying* money, the profit to a person or institution who lends you money, whether on a credit card, a vehicle purchase, business loan, line of credit, or home mortgage.

Usually when you use someone else's money, you pay them back the money you use (principal) plus the charge for the money you use (interest). Some people even equate the percentages to points. As with a mortgage payment, which is an amortized loan, you pay the majority of the lender's interest *first* before you pay any of the principal. This may take several years at the beginning of the loan repayment and, if your property does not increase in value, there will be no equity in the property if you have to sell it to try to profit for yourself. Sometimes, we opt to pay off the principle balance instead of paying the interest, taking more money out of our pockets to pay off the lender. We focus on the lender versus our own families and ourselves.

If you look at life from the HuE-LOC side, you would build a bank of funds to use when issues arise, like major purchases, day-to-day purchases, covering emergencies, college funding, and managing life issues. With a HuE-LOC, you build habits that can bring most interest payments back to you that you would ordinarily pay to banks and financial institutions. Also, as a business owner, you could create a bank of funds to use to capitalize your business without the aid of financial institutions, all while creating efficiencies that optimizes tax benefits for the business and you personally.

No more using other people's money unless you choose to or need to use it. You could be in total control in any economy. You would create options when considering the need for capital for your business. A HuE-LOC strategy gives you the freedom to control the interest you pay to other institutions. If you can control it then you can benefit from it and not everyone else.

Let's consider the facts! We pay out about 34% of our money annually in interest on money we buy. This could make us a slave to the credit score system (credit bureaus) designed as a guide for companies when deciding to whom they will or will not extend credit. History shows us how the consumer credit revolution began after the Great Depression, even then working class people were not able to borrow money in the beginning; it was only for the wealthy. This phenomenon came from the opportunities banks found to loan money and when credit card companies were formed. Ask your grandparents or great-grandparents how they managed their affairs without the credit score system. They had two options: 1) save up the money or 2) be disciplined enough to control what they spent to be able to meet their daily needs and future needs. Oh, and if Mr. Jones at the corner store extended credit, they had to keep a good relationship with him or he could ask them to pay the entire bill at once or offer no credit at all. All while our income is usually finite. However, by paying things off consistently, you could control the interest paid to Mr. Jones, and manage additional money going out from your family.

Here's a tip: Even when you can borrow (buy) your money with no interest due for twelve or thirty-six months or whenever the company's program allows since you have good credit, you are giving money to these institutions for them to use to earn interest, while you are giving the rights away for you to earn interest on that same money called "opportunity cost." The optimal way of working this out is to be able to earn interest on your money while you use that same money to buy things using the programs these companies offer to your advantage.

Remember, interest is profit for another person, company, or bank who receives the interest when you *buy* money from them. They set the terms and you are locked into those terms until the total balance, plus interest, is paid back. If you can find a way to control interest going out, and create more interest coming in to you, then you begin a habit of controlling your *wealth!* You get to keep more money on your side to either keep growing it or be able to build a wealth foundation to do more for you and your family. Become positively selfish.

Eliminate All Debt

Eliminate All Debt

8

Debt is another one of those dreadful words like taxes. No one likes to be in debt or to owe someone else. Debt is the equivalent of being in a financial prison. The debtor decides everything with regards to the deal—how much, when to payback, how much to payback, late charges, and at what date to pay it in full. They even decide the consequences if you don't pay it back. Debt can be hell. There is an entire industry around debt called banking. We all find ourselves, at times, wanting to escape debt, but don't have the slightest clue how to do it. We pay it off then get right back into it. There are also people who feel like debt is their friend; they will always have debt, debt is necessary to operate. They manage debt. Others feel there is good debt and bad debt. I consider debt a form of control and I believe debt should be a choice to leverage when necessary and control the institutions that sell debt instruments.

There are so many forms of debt, but the debt we hear about often are student loans, credit cards, car loans, home loans, home equity lines of credit, business loans, pay day loans, and medical bills. Then there are the common everyday debts, such as utility bills, cable bills, car insurance, homeowner's insurance, and cell phone bills. Although we do not call them debt instruments, paying them is an obligation. Do you remember when cable was a luxury and cellphones were not a necessity? We used to have a choice to have them or not. Although cable competes with free streaming video options and cellphones compete with very few options, we still pay a ton of money to these companies for using these services. If we don't pay them what we owe, it becomes a debt that negatively affects your credit score, hurting your ability to borrow for new services in the future.

Being in debt is not fun. Even having the money to pay the debt, while being under an endless obligation, is not fun. It's like living life to pay someone else. We have to strategize so we don't live a life where it appears that being in debt is the only way to survive without going under. However, I have to stress that being in debt is also a *choice* because there are other options. You can make sacrifices to save money and not allow temptation by salespersons, television, the Internet, and the Jones' (neighbors and friends) to buy things you cannot afford nor do not need. In today's world, we find ourselves pulled into having to have everything we see as if that is what the American dream is all about. The dream is to control your life and the life of your family for years to come in the future.

Savings might not be the current traditional debt eliminator, but it does work. However, if you build a HuE-LOC, you can save money, build an asset, pay off your debt, and eliminate debt all together. While doing this you can simultaneously build and grow your money so it helps you make decisions above borrowing money from others as if it is the standard. Be in control, stay in control. This can also eliminate the need to have to get a loan or use a credit card when emergencies or major purchases are required. What about an alternative of using the credit cards to earn points for benefits and being able to pay the card off before the thirty days and interest accruing with money from your HuE-LOC? What about controlling the use of credit card debt for a great credit score, collecting reward points, and using your HuE-LOC to leverage its power to stay in control? The bottom line is learning the importance of discipline and focus, while setting up and building your HuE-LOC. This, my friend, is the power of the Human Equity Line of Credit™.

My client, Tina, always felt like debt was something she needed to have to operate in life, ever since going to college where she received her first credit card without even having any credit history or a job. Tina felt like she must keep good credit to borrow money to do anything in this world. However, she never learned about money management strategies. Even after landing her first job on her path to her career, it was all about getting more credit to manage major purchases, handle day-to-day expenses, and to be able to create the status she saw friends, colleagues, and family members experience. Get that platinum or black card; get that loan for the Mercedes or BMW, or that first mortgage loan as soon as possible to catch up with others in her peer group. Like most, Tina did not have any money management training; it was just easy to follow the footprints everyone else made. It was not long before there was a recession to change the income coming in to cover all her early debts. This can wipe out income and savings, which for most is a reactive situation not proactive. However, Tina also thinks she can use her retirement plans (401(k), 403b, 457) as a savings tool. She also realizes how much money is lost with this tool as a place to go to for money prior to age 59 ½, where there is a 10% tax penalty right off the bat plus taxes. Now realizing even this tool was not the most optimal place to get money. Tina now wonders, with all the bills she has, how she can save for a rainy day while saving for retirement.

The idea of living below your means, with all the consumer stimulation in the universe driving our emotions to spend, pulls against the very nature of building a life. Tina had to make changes and sacrifices. She realized she needed to step back to find money management training.

Most people think a relationship with a bank is the only way to manage their funds. Even with the advent of PayPal, Square up, Venmo, Cash App, etc., we must know how this fits in our personal finance picture. We must know where each tool fits on our Money Pyramid (bonus section).

Groups like Money Mastery (Moneymastery.com) are helping people learn money management strategies through a system that shows you how to figure out each day, each month, what you should be spending, setting goals for now, and your future needs of money. Since cashflow needs are never-ending. Tina decided to stop flying by the seat of her pants and get a structure for this thing called money. We earn it, but do we keep it or manage it during our lifetime? She also found that there were places to rest money, save it, grow it, use it, control it, for a lifetime, and create goals and plans that are in her favor, being able to choose debt instruments to enhance her life not to be in control of her life. The HuE-LOC played a strong role. Once she educated herself, she started teaching it to her family and friends.

Manage *Personal* and *Business* Affairs with Ease in *Any* Economy

Manage *Personal* and *Business* Affairs with Ease in *Any* Economy

9

L ive long enough and your generation will experience different economies—up, down and sideways. We love the good economies when things look to be going up and we fear the bad economies when things start to go down or affect us personally, and we sit idol during the sideways economies when things seem quiet and steady and there are no major movements to disrupt our daily lives. These are even economic times when we don't think anything is going on, but should be the times when we really prepare for an upswing or downturn in the economy to be able to handle it better. It is all about being aware and proactive. Make hay when the sun shines.

During my lifetime, I have witnessed my fair share of economic ups, downs, and sideways and now I can talk about it and share things that can help you manage. Why do most of us react to these changes? Why can't we become proactive in our efforts and manage any economy that comes our way? We should be able to buy when everybody is selling and sell when everybody is buying. Wealthy people live above economies and only feel the downsides very little, but put themselves in a position to buy on the lows and take advantage of upswings in the world. We do not have to be uber wealthy to be proactive. I am not saying that the economy doesn't have its hiccups that will catch us off guard because a lot of change occurs without our knowledge and by the time it occurs, it started months, if not years, before we feel it directly in our pockets. We may also just be getting started in our adult careers. But, what I do know is that when you establish your own strategy or your HuE-LOC, a multilayer approach to your own finances, you don't have to rely solely on the state of the economy. You win when economies rise, you manage when economies fall, and you prepare during times when economies are stable.

Economic situations arise daily and are simply a part of everyday life. When economies move, it can affect how we manage our financial lives. We do have the choice to be proactive or reactive. For the most part, people normally react because economic change is unpredictable. We can become proactive with changes in habits and understanding history.

Change strategies and your habits by choosing money management as a solution for your family's economic future. **Manage the economy and not let the economy manage you.**

We purchase auto insurance, homeowners insurance, and health insurance to manage risk against life events or personal loss. Although law mandates these products, we still budget to have these tools to manage risk, which keep us from having to pay large sums of money out in unforeseen times or circumstances. Life insurance is the *only* insurance that is not mandated by law to purchase. It is traditionally designed to protect income and to manage personal affairs. It just so happens that the contracts on Life Insurance can also be customized to benefit us while we are alive and not just in case of the death of the insured. We must learn and look to these tools and strategies we have not considered in the past based on the miseducation or misdirection of life insurance, so our future and the future of our families are better off. Again, I have to continue emphasizing that the key to financial and economic freedom is building a HuE-LOC.

You do not have to succumb to economic changes when you become a "Change Agent!"

Enhance and Guarantee Retirement

Enhance and Guarantee Retirement

10

A secure, comfortable retirement should be at the forefront of everyone's mind, which presents the ultimate in goals to work for during a lifetime. Retirement does not mean to stop working; it means to be in control of your ability to manage money so you can own your time and decide how you want to live. When you go out every day to bring in income, you are filling your buckets during your accumulation years. The retirement years are your distribution years, which are the years you will be spending your wealth, while enjoying your life. For many, the thought of making it from one day to the next is a stretch and making retirement a priority is somewhere far in the future or not a consideration at all. There will come a time in life where clocking into a job or working a business will not be your choice of things to do when you wake up. This could come because of personal choice, age, illness, an employer decision, or emergency. Therefore, being financially prepared is a must. It would be sad to work a lifetime only to approach retirement years and not be able to live good or take care of yourself the way you had been while you were working. It is estimated that a couple will need at least $250,000 just for healthcare expense in retirement. Also, people will be living longer based on modern medicine. As a result, actuaries are lowering insurance rates by almost 30%. All of our goals should be to allow our money to outlive us. This means we had the use of it through our entire life and are able to teach and leave a financial foundation for your family or even an institution of your choice.

Through the HuE-LOC program, you are putting money directly into a retirement bucket based on tax advantages and protections for you and your family and not just into government-based programs such as a 401(k), 403(b), 457, or a thrift savings plan. Building a HuE-LOC affords you the opportunity to enhance, as well as guarantee income that you can use during the accumulation phase, and the distribution phase of your life. We must consider a future potential state of the economy, our tax positions, our health, our lifestyles, and future expenses. Retirement is a time to relax, relate, and release from all your years of hard work. It is a time to find relief from stress and pressure. Create your own terms. Build your tax-free bucket.

Become Your
Own Bank

Become Your Own Bank

Becoming your own bank is a process and strategy to put you in control of your financial life. Becoming a bank means operating similar to the banking process with which you are familiar, where most of our money resides. We understand financial institutions, government rules and regulations around banking as customers, which drive how we manage our daily lives. Most, if not all, of these rules are forced upon us and we have to react to them. Ever read the new terms and conditions information mailed to you by your bank? Probably not! However, this process to become your own bank does not mean to get a charter from the Federal Reserve or sanctioned by the state and federal government to set up a commercial banking system. Simply put, becoming your own bank is a habit-changing strategy to set up how you and your family manage money against the normal rules and regulations that we have become so used to. An example would be if you and your family have a place to hold money, allow it to grow, while using it for anything including loaning it out and possibly for other investments. With a slew of other benefits for *your* banking system, it naturally sets up to leave money for the next generations.

Joe, entrepreneur/small business owner, makes money by selling online. He earns weekly revenue and income. He has his money going into to a commercial bank/credit union, like any other business owner. If he needs a loan, he has to apply for a loan with the bank, or he could use his own money from his account, taking it away from earning any money the bank promises for parking his money in the account. He has to make a choice to do one thing or the other. If he sets up a High Cash Value Whole Life Insurance policy as a base tool for the HuE-LOC, where he can park his money—*his bank*, allow it to grow compounded, gain potential additional dividends, and be able to borrow money without any payback rules or credit requirements involved, essentially allowing an entrepreneur like Joe to be able to be in control of his money for his business and still grow money he is making. Making money with an "and" strategy not and "or" only choice.

Teaching those ways to our children and grandchildren, not only ensure our life but also, the lives of upcoming generations teaching them to think alternatively as it relates to money. The HuE-LOC is your bank that fits your current situation no matter what age or time in life. No matter your income, you can start investing in YOU with your own money by building a HuE-LOC. As your own bank:

- You make the decisions
- You assign interest rates for loans
- You set the terms
- There is no FDIC oversight
- There has been no need for bailouts
- You manage financial habits
- You will be an honest banker because you will be the customer and the bank.
- Funds are creditor-proof
- You customize your bank

Help Family, Church Members, and Employees *Learn* to Build a HuE-LOC

Help Family, Church Members, and Employees *Learn* to Build a HuE-LOC

12

Knowledge is power! Having the know-how and the skills to produce change—and then to change habits—is priceless. Every day, people seek a quick fix to financial freedom. I am sorry to be the bearer of bad news, but there is none. You can even tell me if you make substantially more money, or even win the lottery that your problems will be solved, but with the same bad habits, it just creates the same issues, but only bigger. Money accumulated quickly without understanding and habit changes does not usually last. We want to learn to be good stewards of our money; teaching those around us to begin the process of building generational wealth. Teaching the Money Pyramid where each product goes in our financial foundation.

Wealthy families, major corporations, and even banks have utilized these tier-one investment strategies for years to build their fortunes. Their wealth is generational—current and future generations will be financially secure because they trusted the process. We need to teach this strategy to young people, families, in schools, in colleges, in companies, and to entrepreneurs.

Our children need to learn the foundation of building wealth at a young age, creating healthy money habits, even if they babysit or have a lemonade stand. We must be willing to share this knowledge so everyone can thrive and possess financial freedom. Aren't you tired of being a slave to money, debt, and economic issues? This is the time for you to ask yourself some hard questions.

▶ Who taught you how to manage money?

▶ Do you know how to manage money when it is in your hands?

▶ Do you track your spending to control it?

▶ Do you use a commercial bank to hold your money until you spend it?

▶ Do you have three buckets of savings—lifestyle, emergency, and retirement?

▶ Are you looking at the big picture things that could happen in the world, the nation, local economy, and personal life to become proactive with your finances?

▶ Are you using credit cards or debt instruments like a home equity line of credit to manage your life? Literally managing your life with debt.

▶ Are you paying taxes as a foregone conclusion?

▶ Do you think of earning more interest than paying?

▶ Do you have healthy or unhealthy spending habits based on emotions, motivations, history, and maybe the pressures of peers and other life factors?

▶ Is money management a real priority of yours throughout your life?

These questions we often avoid, not willing to think about them; we have created habits we do not want to think are inefficient ways of doing things. Simply because we believe they have worked for us. Remember, habits are what we do knowingly or unknowingly that become the norm without challenging and testing the options to change. I have heard it takes twenty-one days to change a habit, a diet, an exercise routine, and maybe even a way of managing our money so we get the most of it throughout our life. First, we must be willing and interested in learning something different that may go against our routine. Would you have taken classes to get an associate's degree in money management, additional to your degree in a career field at the bachelor's degree level? Should it have been a mandatory course? If you answered yes then you could have already created habits based on money management strategies and wealth building. You would have used this information for your first job out of college. We must not be afraid to know there has to be another way that others have used differently to become wealthy, sustaining positive finances, and building strong legacies.

When I believe I am in an impossible situation, I always ask myself, "Has *anybody ever* been in my exact situation and become wildly successful?"

I don't care what your situation is, there is a solution, and it is up to you to find out what it is and how the other person made it out.

Let's change our habits and change our lives. Let's build a HuE-LOC. Then we can help each other.

Pass Your HuE-LOC Down to Your Children and Grandchildren

Pass Your HuE-LOC Down to Your Children and Grandchildren

13

Proverbs 13:22 (NIV) says, *A good man or woman leaves an inheritance to his children's children.* King Solomon, one of the wisest men ever, wrote this Proverb and it still stands solid today. If a man can leave an inheritance where his family doesn't have to struggle and has something to build upon for life, it is honorable. This also does not mean you don't have a good life yourself.

The HuE-LOC is a *pay-it-forward* plan, so your children and grandchildren will not have to break their backs for a financially secure life, rely on the government, or drown in debt because they have no other options. Building a HuE-LOC will afford you the opportunity to live financially free today and still have some for tomorrow. Don't believe what elected officials say about leaving trillions of dollars of debt to our children and grandchildren. If you think your elected officials will allow their children and grandchildren to suffer, you had better think again. They are familiar with this strategy. You can change this for your own families by changing your habits now to protect your lives and the lives of your children and grandchildren; giving them a leg up when it is time for them to help with your senior care. It will become routine in your family and much appreciated by your children. In addition, they will want to help you because you made a way for them to make it as well. Become a *legacy starter* and a *legacy changer*.

If you are ready to build a Human Equity Line of Credit™, no matter your age or finances, visit www. humanequitylineofcredit.com, complete the online form, and an agent will contact you as soon as possible.

Bonus

MONEY PYRAMID

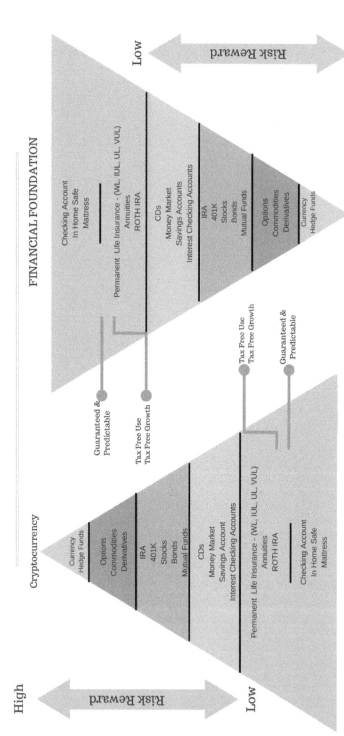

Money Pyramid

Left Pyramid

Financial foundation based on a triangle or Egyptian pyramid is the strongest point of the shape. The base is where we should concentrate our safe and predictable money for handling all of life's everyday events and unforeseen circumstances where we need money to be available immediately.

As you move up the pyramid, you are putting more money at risk. Although the risk starts out to be minor, it is still controlled by other institutions and the outcomes are determined via the financial instrument or it is undetermined, but speculated by historical evidence. The central theme is that taxes are involved when there are profits and growth of your funds.

The pyramid is angled on both sides, so you have a smaller percentage of your funds in these riskier vehicles as you go up the pyramid. The predictable and guaranteed funds stay at the bottom, so you cannot tip over your pyramid.

As your pyramid base grows wider, by percentage, you will have more money available for riskier vehicles where the reward is higher, but so are the risks. If you follow the money pyramid, you know where most products fit, which end up being the tools to build your pyramid as big as your dreams can conceive.

Right Pyramid

This inverted money pyramid shows how a large number of people use their tools. They take income that comes into the base of the pyramid and invest straight into risk tools that are restrictive. They keep what's left in guaranteed and predictable until it is time to spend it on unforeseen and unpredictable events in life. This is never a way to build a pyramid. At any time, when our riskier vehicles lose money, our pyramid falls over. If they win money then our money goes into our upside down base and it falls over anyway.

The money pyramid is a framework to where products that are being sold to us every day can be placed so we can make sure we are building so we can stay on sure footing for different economies, emergencies, opportunities, events, etc. We must live for the long haul and not just for today.

Landing Your Airplane to Retirement

G oing into retirement is like landing an airplane and easing into later stages of life while setting the wheels down nice and smooth. Landing your airplane of retirement shouldn't be a sudden event, or you could crash land.

Before your flight (life) takes off, as the pilot, you check and learn everything about your airplane's engine and its inner workings to ensure a smooth takeoff, which is exactly the same strategy when we start school as youth all the way through high school, college, and the many professions available to us.

With a known destination before flying (goal setting), we are left to ponder on what our experiences will be along the way and the successes we plan to have throughout life.

When we pick up speed on the runway and lift-off, we start to fly and this is when we begin to earn our first paycheck (income). As we ascend, we learn that there are winds pushing against us like taxes, social security, retirement plans, insurance, finances, student loans, rent, mortgage, entertainment, food, clothing, and shelter. All coming from our one income. All while learning how to spend.

As we climb up to a comfortable altitude, where the airplane glides very easy and the winds are smooth, we encounter clouds, which may impede our visibility as we move through the early stages in life. Clouds can represent us having to make lots of financial decisions and learning from them as we live day to day. How do we make these decisions? Who do we turn to, or do we just figure it out?

At the highest altitude, we may encounter more wind by getting married, having children, buying a house, and enjoying life, which tends to make us adjust our airplane. We must begin to think more directly about our decision, continue to learn how things work and take more assessments of our flight pattern and plans. We have to keep our airplane flying straight to our original and future goals

We get used to the new altitudes and situations keeping the airplane flying straight through our thirties and forties. Dealing with life events known and unknown and economies that we can and cannot predict.

However, when we reach our fifties, we begin thinking we must consider what it looks like to land our airplane. What preparation do we need to make should we tighten our seat belt, let our seats up and lock our tray tables in position? Or, do we need to fly a little higher or longer to land our airplane safely to meet our goals? Remember, we came through some known and unknown times in life.

As we decide to land the airplane, we tell everyone to buckle up. It is important to make sure we retire properly and let everyone know we will be landing very soon.

So the next time you fly, think of where the airplane is in your life, and how you are preparing to land it in retirement. No matter how high you are flying, you must prepare to come down, and it should be as smooth as the takeoff.

Build Your HuE-LOC
Steven E. LaBroi

Affirmations for Building a
HUMAN EQUITY LINE OF CREDIT LIFE

I believe in NO DEBT and true wealth

I believe in stress free lifestyle paying limited
taxes and minimal interest

I believe in consuming as a real choice not a
compelled action

I believe in generational intelligence and moving
information forward to my network and family

I believe in changing the paradigm of wealth building
for my family and teaching others

I believe in creating great lives for future generations
by creating new traditions and legacy building

I believe in creating financial tools for my income
while I am living and pass along those tools with
wealth to the next three generations

ABOUT THE AUTHOR

Focused, passionate, and one who delivers on his commitments, STEVEN E. LABROI is the Chief Strategist of the LaBroi Insurance Group, LLC, a nationwide insurance strategy firm, President and CEO of Sales4us.com, Inc., a small business sales consulting firm, and the executive producer of the film *Things Never Said*, starring the star of STARZ hit show, *Power*, Omari Hardwick, and *Shameless* star, Shanola Hampton.

Dedicated to the financial services industry, LaBroi is a graduate of Morehouse College in Atlanta, Georgia, with a bachelor's in finance and banking. He resides in Washington, DC, where he is committed to teaching others the valuable strategies he has learned throughout his life to maintain and manage personal finances.

For speaking engagements and group purchases, please contact Steven E. LaBroi at:

On the web: www.stevenlabroi.com
Via email: teachhueloc@stevenlabroi.com
Phone: 202-544-6226

CPSIA information can be obtained
at www.ICGtesting.com
Printed in the USA
BVHW091318040222
627987BV00008B/496

9 780983 435440